Journey Through Arabia

Andy Hopkins

Level 2

Series Editors: Andy Hopkins and Jocelyn Potter

Pearson Education Limited
Edinburgh Gate, Harlow,
Essex CM20 2JE, England
and Associated Companies throughout the world.

ISBN: 978-1-292-19600-8

This edition first published by Pearson Education Ltd 2013

1 3 5 7 9 10 8 6 4 2

Text copyright © Andy Hopkins 2013

Illustrations by Ollie Cuthbertson

The moral rights of the authors have been asserted in accordance with
the Copyright Designs and Patents Act 1988

Set in 12/15.5pt A. Garamond
Printed in China
SWTC/01

Published by Pearson Education Ltd

Acknowledgements
The publisher would like to thank the following for their kind permission
to reproduce their photographs:

(Key: b-bottom; c-centre; l-left; r-right; t-top)

Corbis: Eric Lafforgue / Arabianeye 27

All other images © Pearson Education

*Every effort has been made to trace the copyright holders and we apologise in advance for any unintentional omissions.
We would be pleased to insert the appropriate acknowledgement in any subsequent edition of this publication.*

For a complete list of the titles available in the Pearson English Active Readers series, visit www.pearsonenglishactivereaders.com.
Alternatively, write to your local Pearson Education office or to
Pearson English Readers Marketing Department, Pearson Education, Edinburgh Gate, Harlow, Essex CM20 2JE, England.

Contents

1.1 What's the book about?

The people and places in this story are in Arabia, but in an earlier time. Look at this picture. Discuss with another student a journey across this country now. Think about these questions:

1 How can you do it?
2 What will you take?
3 Will it be easy? Why (not)?
4 Will it be dangerous? Why (not)?

1.2 What happens first?

1 **What do you think? Look at the picture on page 2.**

   a What are the people doing?
   b Where are the boats going to and from?
   c What is in the bags?

2 **Now look at the map on page 7. Are these sentences right (✓) or wrong (✗)?**

   a Ships came to Arabia from India.

   b The journey in this story starts from Marib.

   c The journey goes north to Gaza.

   d It follows the mountains.

   e Gaza and Alexandria are on the Red Sea.

CHAPTER 1

The Journey Begins

The camels start to get up too: back legs first, then the front legs.
They make a lot of noise. The long journey is starting again ...

The sun is going down on an autumn afternoon. There is a light wind. I look round at the people and the animals: four hundred **camels**, my uncle said, and about 120 people. There is colour everywhere – on people's clothes, on the camel bags. But the people and the animals are quiet now. They are waiting for something.

And then I hear it. A shout comes from the front: 'Let's go! Let's go!' It is my uncle.

Slowly, everybody begins to move. The men and boys get to their feet. The camels start to get up too: back legs first, then the front legs. They make a lot of noise. The long journey is starting again, and the bags across the camels' backs are heavy. But there is a beautiful **smell**, because in the bags there are **spices** from India and the East, and **incense** from the south of Arabia.

'Is it your first time with the **caravan**?' asks a boy. He is a little older than me.

'Yes, it is,' I answer.

'Your uncle is an important man. And he's good at his job. He knows the best ways through the mountains and across the **desert**, and everybody listens to him. Are you afraid of the journey?'

I look at him. 'No, I'm not afraid. But everything's new to me.'

---

camel /ˈkæməl/ (n) A *camel* is a large animal. It can live in very dry countries and can carry people on its back
smell /smel/ (n/v) Some flowers have a beautiful *smell*. They *smell* beautiful.
You *smell* things with your nose.
spice /spaɪs/ (n) We use *spices* in food. They make food nicer and more interesting.
incense /ˈɪnsens/ (n) You can use *incense* when you want a lovely smell in a building.
caravan /ˈkærəvæn/ (n) In a *caravan* there are many people and animals on a long journey.
In past times, *caravans* often stopped at **caravanserais**. People and animals slept there.
desert /ˈdezət/ (n) A *desert* is a large, very dry place. The Sahara is a *desert* in North Africa.

'You can ask me for help.' He smiles. 'My name's Hassan.'
'Hello, Hassan. I'm Yazid.'

◆

The boys' families live in Qana, a large city by the sea in the south of
Arabia. Ships go to India from there. They take incense, and bring
back spices and **gold**. Other ships bring incense from Dhofar and from
Somalia. The best incense in the world comes from Dhofar.

gold /gəʊld/ (n) *Gold* is yellow and comes from the ground. It is very expensive. Some
people have *gold* teeth.

2

Spices from the East

Spices from the East arrived in Qana by sea. Here are some of the most important spices. People in many countries cook with them today.

Cardamom
In some Arab countries, people put cardamom in coffee.

Ginger
In winter, Arabs put ginger in hot milk.

Pepper
Today, one fifth of the world's spice **trade** is in pepper.

Cinnamon
In the past, cinnamon was more expensive than gold. The Egyptians used it when they **buried** people.

trade /treɪd/ (n/v) The spice *trade* is the buying and selling of spices, inside or between countries. **Traders** buy and sell things; they *trade* them.
bury /ˈberi/ (v) When people die, we usually *bury* them in the ground.

Yazid's and Hassan's families are traders. They take incense and spices north by caravan to Egypt and to Gaza, on the Mediterranean Sea. From there, the incense and spices go to Europe.

The caravan is beginning a journey north from Qana. It will be months before it arrives at the Mediterranean Sea. The people in the caravan are all traders; they buy and sell. The Greeks, the Romans, the Egyptians and other people near the Mediterranean love spices and incense from Arabia and the East. They will pay a lot of money for them.

◆

'How many hours do we **travel** in a day, Hassan?' I ask.

'Usually about eight or ten hours,' he says. 'And we move in the evenings and at night. It isn't hot then, and the camels like it better.'

'And where do we stop?' I ask.

'We have to find water for the camels,' Hassan says. 'The animals are very important to the caravan. Without them, we can't do anything. The camels can drink in about sixty or seventy places on the way – in villages, in the desert, and sometimes in cities. Usually, we stop at one of those places. At other times, we stop in the desert and sleep. It's a long journey. It takes more than three months.'

'Three months? That *is* a long time!'

'Yes, and of course the journey home takes three months too,' says Hassan with a smile. 'The journey north is difficult. The caravan has to go through mountains and across desert. In the mountains there's a lot of water and food for the animals, but the desert is very dry. Your uncle Sayf knows the best places. He has to find those places again and again, because without food and water everybody will die.'

My uncle calls me. 'Yazid, come up to the front with me,' he shouts.

'You're going to see some wonderful places,' my uncle tells me. 'We're going through the mountains to famous cities. First to Shabwa, then to Timna, then Marib, the richest city in Saba. We'll stop at all of them for one or two days. More traders will travel with our caravan from those

travel /ˈtrævəl/ (v) When you *travel*, you go from one place to another place, often on a long journey.

Incense: frankincense and myrrh

Frankincense is a white **resin** from trees in the south of Arabia. Two or three times each year, people make cuts in the tree. Then the resin comes out and goes hard. In a fire, it has a beautiful smell.

Myrrh resin is red or yellow, or sometimes black. It comes from trees in the south of Arabia and from Somalia. Egyptians used it when they buried people. Everything smells better with frankincense and myrrh.

At the time of this story, everybody wanted frankincense and myrrh, so they were very expensive. They cost more than gold. Arabia traded about 1,500,000 kilos of frankincense and about 400,000 kilos of myrrh every year.

resin /ˈrezɪn/ (n) *Resin* runs out of some trees when you cut them. It is thicker than water.

cities. The journey is easier with a lot of people, because it's sometimes dangerous.'

'Why is Marib a rich city?' I ask him.

'Because it's one of the centres of the frankincense trade,' he says. 'And also because every trader, from the south and the north, travels through Marib. And everybody has to pay for that.'

'Pay? Why?' I ask.

'When we traders travel through a country or a city, we always have to pay,' my uncle tells me. 'This caravan is expensive. We also have to buy food for the animals, of course. We have to eat and drink. And we all have to sleep somewhere.'

The caravan moves slowly through the mountains.

'It's beautiful near Marib – very green. The people there have a lot of water, so there's a lot of food in their **fields**. And there's a famous **dam** there. You have to see it,' my uncle tells me with a smile.

field /fiːld/ (n) A *field* is a big, open place in the country for vegetables and other food or for animals.

dam /dæm/ (n) A *dam* is a big wall across a river.

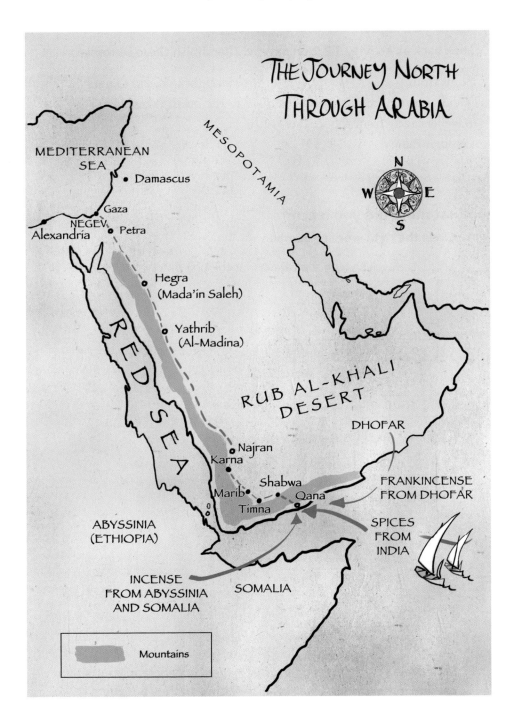

2.1 Were you right?

Look back at Activity 1.2.2 on page iv. Then finish these sentences.

Ships from [1]................................ brought spices to Qana.
Yazid's journey begins there. The road to the north takes the
travellers away from the sea, across the [2]................................ and
through the [3]................................ . They are going to Gaza, on the
[4]................................ Sea.

2.2 What more did you learn?

1 Circle the right word or number.

a ..... is travelling with the caravan for the first time.

> Yazid Hassan Sayf

b His family are ..... .

> cooks doctors traders

c The caravan travels for ..... hours a day.

> 8–10 6–8 4–6

d The journey will take about ..... weeks each way.

> 3 6 12

e Frankincense and myrrh come from ..... .

> flowers trees underground

f ..... was the richest city in Saba.

> Shabwa Marib Timna

g There was a famous ..... in Marib.

> desert building dam

2 Look again at the spices on page 3. Which do people in your country use when they cook? What food and drink do they put them in?

2.3 Language in use

Look at the sentences in the box.
Then write sentences with *have to*.

> We **have to** find water for the camels.
>
> The caravan **has to** go through mountains ...

1 Sayf / find water for the camels.

....

2 Many of the travellers / walk.

....

3 they / go through the mountains?

....

4 Why / we / stop here?

....

5 The camels don't / drink every day.

....

2.4 What happens next?

Discuss these questions. What do you think?

1 Which of these sentences about Marib are right (✔)?

   a ◯   Marib was a big city.   **c** ◯   It had a lot of rain.

   b ◯   It was very rich.   **d** ◯   It was high in the mountains.

2 Why was this woman famous?

Queen of Sheba

9

The City of the Queen of Sheba

I look to my right: big houses, green fields and water. I look to
my left: more houses, more trees and plants, more water!

Night after night, the caravan climbs higher into the mountains.
It stops at towns and villages. Then the travellers go over the top
and, day after day, climb slowly down from three thousand metres to
the desert below. They stop at the famous cities of Shabwa and Timna,
and other traders travel with them from there. Then the road takes them
north-west between the mountains and the desert. They are now twenty
days and nights from Qana. They can see green fields with trees and
plants everywhere.

The caravan moves slowly round a large **rock.** Suddenly, from the
front, somebody shouts, 'There it is. Marib!'

plant /plɑːnt/ (n/v) Trees and flowers are *plants*. You *plant* a tree when you put it in the
ground.
rock /rɒk/ (n) When you cut into a mountain, you find *rock*. You can see *rocks* on **rocky**
ground; they are hard and heavy.

An hour later, I can see the high walls of a big city. Inside the walls there are tall houses, thousands of them. Outside, the morning sun is shining on water.

'What's that, Hassan?' I ask. 'Is it a river?'

'No,' he answers. 'It's the water from the dam. It goes down from the dam onto the fields and makes them green.'

I look to my right: big houses, green fields and water. I look to my left: more houses, more trees and plants, more water! It's wonderful. It's a beautiful place.

◆

Marib is the most important city in the **Kingdom** of Saba. It sits at the foot of high mountains, next to the desert. There is usually not much rain here, but two times every year, for about two months, it rains heavily. The rainwater comes down from the mountains and goes into the dry river bed. Then it runs to the great Marib Dam and stops. From the dam, small rivers of water go out to the fields near the city.

The Great Marib Dam

Who built the dam? And when? We don't know. But we do know that there was a dam there in about 790 BCE*. This dam was a big wall 580 metres long and four metres high. In places, the wall was eight metres thick. Later, people made the wall bigger. At its highest it was fourteen metres. The great dam broke many times over the next thousand years and people built it up again and again. But in about 570 CE* there was a big **earthquake**. It brought the wall down. People could not build it again; it was too difficult. Without a dam, there was no water for the fields. With no food for their animals, the people of Marib left the city.

*BCE/CE: years before/after the year 0

king /kɪŋ/ (n) The *king* is the most important person in some countries. Usually, his father was also the *king*. A *king's* country is his **kingdom**.
earthquake /ˈɜːθkweɪk/ (n) When there is an *earthquake*, the ground moves. In a strong *earthquake*, buildings fall.

I am with my uncle again. The city walls of Marib are nearer now.

'The road to the north is very long, Uncle. How do you know the way?' I ask.

My uncle is quiet for a minute, then he speaks. 'We know the way north from the sun and the night sky. We follow the road between the desert and the mountains. We don't go a long way into the desert, because there's no water there. And we travel in the high mountains as little as possible. The road through the mountains is difficult and dangerous, and there are **bandits**. They wait for caravans and take everything. Often, they kill people.'

'So we always try to stop in a place with other people?' I ask.

'Yes. The people in the villages and towns on the road help the traders and their caravans. They have food and beds for us. But there's another thing too – the most important thing of all.'

'What's that?' I ask.

'Towns are always near water,' my uncle says. 'People can't live without water! And you find water at the foot of these mountains. The best way to the north stays near the mountains. Most people think that there are a hundred ways north. But there aren't really many ways. All caravans have to follow the water.'

bandit /ˈbændɪt/ (n) *Bandits* wait near roads. Then they take things from travellers.

Queen Bilqis – The Queen of Sheba

There are many stories about **Queen** Bilqis of Marib, the queen of the rich country of Saba (Sheba). She was a very beautiful and strong woman. People say that King Solomon invited her to Jerusalem – more than one thousand years before our story. She made the long journey over the mountains and across the desert, and she took incense, spices and gold to the King. They say that her caravan had 797 camels and other animals.

The Queen travelled on a bed of gold, on a beautiful white camel. On the long journey, the caravan had to leave Saba and travel through other countries. The Queen met their kings, and perhaps this was the beginning of the incense road.

Some stories say that Queen Bilqis had a child with King Solomon. When the child got older, he was King Menelik of Ethiopia. All future Ethiopian kings and queens were, some people say, from the family of Queen Bilqis.

queen /kwiːn/ (n) The *queen* is the most important person in some countries. In some other countries, she is the wife of the king.

3.1 Were you right?

Look back at your answers to Activity 2.4.1. Then choose words below and write about Marib.

Marib is a ¹................... city. It is in the kingdom of ²................... . The city is ³................... the desert, ⁴................... high mountains. Rainwater runs down from the ⁵................... to the dam. A lot of caravans go through Marib. These caravans make Marib a ⁶................... city.

1 small big new	4 in on below
2 Saba Shabwa Timna	5 fields mountains houses
3 in next to below	6 rich high beautiful

3.2 What more did you learn?

1 Put these in the right order, 1–6.

a ◯ The caravan leaves Qana.   d ◯ It arrives in Marib.

b ◯ It goes down the mountains. e ◯ It climbs up the mountains.

c ◯ It travels to Timna.   f ◯ It stops in Shabwa.

2 Are these sentences right (✔) or wrong (✗)?

a ◯ People built the Marib Dam many times.

b ◯ The city used water from the dam for more than two thousand years.

c ◯ The last dam fell in a big earthquake.

d ◯ The towns on the caravan road were high in the mountains.

e ◯ *Sheba* is another name for *Saba*.

f ◯ Queen Bilqis went north because she wanted to trade with the Roman

g ◯ People think that she had a child with King Solomon.

3.3 Language in use

Look at the sentences in the box. Then write these words in the story below.

between	next to	in front of
to	at	in	near	from
through	across

> The road takes them north-west **between** the mountains and the desert.

> The road **through** the mountains is difficult and dangerous.

I went on a walking holiday with a friend last year. We stayed
¹ ...at... a hotel ² .... the mountains. My friend was in
the room ³ .... mine. There was a river ⁴ .... the
hotel, ⁵ .... us and the mountains. On the first day, we
went ⁶ .... the river ⁷ .... a small boat, and walked
⁸ .... the trees to the foot of the mountains. The walk
⁹ .... the boat ¹⁰ .... the mountains took about an
hour. We walked all day and saw some beautiful places.

3.4 What happens next?

Make notes in your notebook. What do you think?

1 Look at the picture on page 16. What is happening? Who are the people on horses? What do they want?

2 What do you know about camels? Why do they do well in deserts?

CHAPTER 3

Dangerous Nights!

*The men start fighting. There is a lot of noise. We can
see the fighting, and we try to go there ...*

It is the middle of the night. Our caravan is travelling through the desert by the light of the night sky. The high mountains to the west are dark.

Out of the black mountains, men on horses suddenly arrive. They are shouting loudly. There are about twenty of them. They are bandits! Before we can do anything, the bandits are at the back of the caravan. The slowest camels are there, and the slowest travellers.

'Help! My brothers, help me!' a man shouts.

We want to help, but we are near the front of the caravan. The bandits' horses are fast and our camels are slow. The men start fighting.

There is a lot of noise. We can see the fighting, and we try to go there as fast as possible. But we are too late. The horsemen take five of our camels. They have the animals and they have the bags of incense, spices and gold on their backs.

Three of our men are dead.

'What shall we do, Uncle?' I ask. 'Shall we go after the bandits and kill them?'

'No, Yazid. We can't. The night is dark and the mountains are dangerous. We have to bury our brothers and then leave them. We have to get to the next caravanserai as quickly as possible.'

Caravans and caravanserai

A caravanserai was a very large open place with high walls and big doors. There were small shops, and food and water for travellers and their animals. There were places for the camels, and large open rooms for the traders. The traders could sleep on the floors. All towns on the incense road had a caravanserai.

Most caravans travelled across the south of Arabia in the dry months, between September and December. In wetter months, heavy rains often washed away bridges and roads.

Many of the people walked, because then the camels could carry more bags. Most traders travelled with two or three camels. The caravans moved as fast as a camel could walk. In ten hours they could travel about forty kilometres.

The great doors of the caravanserai close behind us and we feel better.

Hassan and I take our camels to the water. The animals put their heads down and drink ... and drink ... and drink. They didn't drink yesterday, so they are very thirsty. Our camels can drink 120 litres of water at one time.

Everybody sits down. This feels good after a long night on the road. But we can't forget our dead brothers.

Somebody calls my uncle's name: 'Sayf Ammar. Where is Sayf Ammar?'

'I'm here!' calls my uncle.

They want him to pay for our stay in the caravanserai.

'How many camels are with you?' asks the man.

'Four hundred and fifty,' my uncle says. 'And 140 people.'

'And how will you pay?' asks the man. 'In gold or frankincense?'

My uncle pays in frankincense.

The camels sit down. The traders make their beds on the floor.

Their bags stay near them, because they don't want to lose their incense and spices. Not everybody sleeps at the same time. Some men stand and watch. Their eyes stay open. It can be dangerous everywhere – outside and inside the walls of the caravanserai.

'Yazid,' my uncle says. 'Can you bring some food for us? There's a shop over there.'

Hassan and I walk across the caravanserai and find a shop.

'Good morning, young men,' the man in the shop says. 'What can I do for you?'

'Good morning,' we answer.

'I have bread. I have fruit and some vegetables. And I have milk. I also have food for your animals. What would you like, my friends?'

We buy bread and fruit. We have milk from our camels. And we have water.

We take the food back to my uncle. Then we sit and enjoy it. Food is wonderful at the end of a long day.

The Arabian Camel – the ship of the desert

A strong camel can carry five hundred kilos on its **back**, but most camels carry about two hundred kilos. Camels usually work for six to eight months of the year.

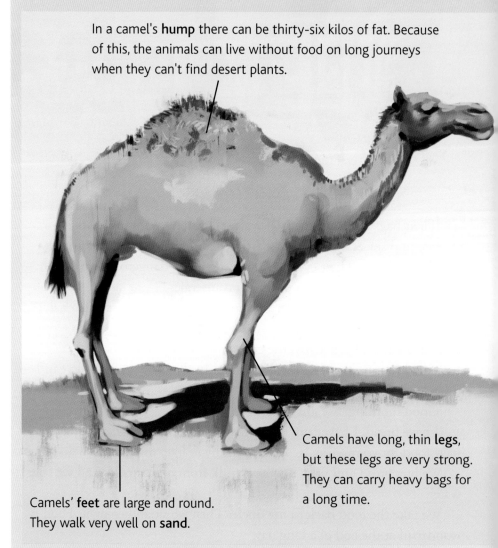

In a camel's **hump** there can be thirty-six kilos of fat. Because of this, the animals can live without food on long journeys when they can't find desert plants.

Camels have long, thin **legs**, but these legs are very strong. They can carry heavy bags for a long time.

Camels' **feet** are large and round. They walk very well on **sand**.

sand /sænd/ (n) You find *sand* on a **sandy** beach or in a desert. When there is a **sandstorm** in the desert, strong winds move the *sand* up from the ground.

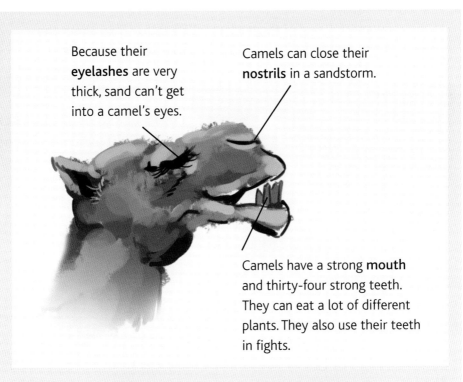

Because their **eyelashes** are very thick, sand can't get into a camel's eyes.

Camels can close their **nostrils** in a sandstorm.

Camels have a strong **mouth** and thirty-four strong teeth. They can eat a lot of different plants. They also use their teeth in fights.

- A large camel can be two metres tall and seven hundred kilos. It can live to about fifty years old.
- Camels can walk for five to seven days without food or water, and they can drink nearly one hundred litres of water in ten minutes.
- A camel carries one baby for about thirteen months before it is born. On its first day, the baby camel opens its eyes and walks. A young camel stays with its mother for five years.
- When a camel has a baby on a journey, people put the baby camel on the back of a large, strong camel. The mother walks behind, and can see her baby at all times.
- Camels have many uses. People of the desert drink their milk. They eat their meat. They make bags from the camels' hair. And, of course, camels can carry people and heavy bags across the desert.

4.1 Were you right?

At the caravanserai, one of the traders tells another man about the bandits. What is wrong with his story? Look back at your notes in Activity 3.4. Then circle the wrong words below. Write new sentences.

> There were about (fifty) bandits. They came at us from across the desert. They were on foot. They killed eight of our brothers. We lost ten camels, with bags of incense, spices and gold.

1 There were about twenty bandits.

2

3

4

5

4.2 What more did you learn?

Write short answers to these questions.

1 How many traders died in the fight with the bandits?   Three

2 Where did the other traders bury them?

3 Why did most caravans travel in the summer?

4 How many kilometres did a caravan travel in an hour?

5 How much water can a camel drink at one time?

6 How does Sayf pay for the caravanserai?

4.3 Language in use

Look at the sentences in the box. Then finish these sentences.

> The **slowest** camels are there, and the **slowest** travellers.

1 Please be as .... *quick* .... (quick) as possible.

2 Hassan is .... (tall) than Yazid.

3 That horse is the .... (fast) of all my horses.

4 Frankincense resin was .... (expensive) than gold, but now it is .... (cheap).

5 Camels are .... (good) than horses in the desert.

6 The Queen of Sheba was the .... (beautiful) woman in the country.

4.4 What happens next?

Look at the pictures in Chapter 4. Discuss these questions. What do you think? Write notes in the box below.

1 What are the people doing in the picture on page 25? What are the camels doing? Why?

2 Look at the pictures of Petra and Hegra on pages 26 and 27. Which countries are they in now?

Notes

Changes

*I look up. My mouth falls open. In front
of me is the most beautiful building.*

After many weeks, our caravan is in Najran. We are leaving Saba and Southern Arabia now.

My uncle and I are looking to the north, with Najran behind us.

'To the east is the biggest sandy desert in Arabia, the Rub Al-Khali,' my uncle tells me. 'We stay away from there. To the west are the mountains. We'll travel this way, to the north, and we'll stay near the foot of those mountains. There's another caravan road from here, Yazid. It goes north-east, round the Rub Al-Khali, to Mesopotamia*. It goes through the wonderful city of Qaryat Dhat Kahil.'

It is late autumn now, but it is hot. On some days, it is 35° in the middle of the day. At night, it is better, at about 15°. We walk slowly across the rocky desert. Will this journey never end? Four weeks later, we go through Yathrib, and then into the country of the Nabateans.

It is very early in the morning and we are about two hours away from the next caravanserai. Usually at this time we can see the sun, but this morning the sky in the east is a dark orange colour.

Hassan is unhappy. 'It doesn't look good, Yazid,' he says. 'The sky's very dark.'

'I can see that, but what does it mean?' I ask.

'A sandstorm is coming this way,' he says.

I watch the sky. Hassan is right. It is getting darker and darker, and the wind is getting stronger too.

The camels move unhappily and make a lot of noise. They know that a sandstorm is coming.

My uncle shouts, 'OK, stop! Get the camels down.'

Most of the animals sit down, but some stay on their feet. They all

*Mesopotamia: now Iraq and other places near the rivers Tigris and Euphrates

turn their faces into the wind and close their eyes.

'Go behind your camel and put your head down,' Hassan tells me.

The wind gets stronger and stronger. The noise of the wind gets louder and louder. The sky is dark now and I can't see anything. There is sand everywhere. It is in my mouth, in my ears, in my eyes.

We stay behind our camels for hours.

Then the wind stops and the caravan can move again.

'Who are the Nabateans?' I ask my uncle an hour or two later.

'They're from the north,' he says, 'and they're traders – very good traders. They're very rich and they build beautiful cities. Their country goes from here to Gaza and Damascus in the north, and to Egypt in the west.'

'But why are they rich?' I ask.

'You know that water is everything in the desert, Yazid. The Nabateans understand water and they can always find it. So they can live in very difficult places in the desert. We can all learn from them. And

the incense road goes through
many of their towns and cities.
All caravans from the south
have to go through Nabatea
and pay its people.'

We walk for many more
weeks. The journey through
the desert is long and hard,
and we are all tired now.
Sometimes we stop at busy
towns. We see some wonderful
things. But my uncle tells me
that our next stop will be at the
most wonderful city of all. It
is the biggest city in Nabatea
– Petra. He looks excited, but
he looks tired too. He is not a
young man now.

The mountains here are red
and look beautiful in the sun.
When we get near the city, we
see green fields of plants and

trees. The caravan moves slowly – and now there is a mountain in front
of us!

'Are we going over this mountain?' I ask Hassan.

Hassan gives a little laugh. 'No. Wait and see, Yazid!'

The front of the caravan turns, and I watch carefully. We take a small
road between two high rocks. There isn't much room for people here.
The camels have to go one after another. In places, we can feel the rock
walls on the left and right with our hands.

After a short time, from behind me, Hassan says, 'Look up, Yazid – in
front of you!'

I look up. My mouth falls open. In front of me is the most beautiful building. People are working on the front of it. They are cutting it out of the rock!

'What is it?' I ask. 'What are they making?

'I think it's for their king. When he dies, they'll bury him in there,' Hassan answers.

Now the streets are very busy.

'They say that thirty thousand people live in Petra!' Hassan tells me.

Some other Nabatean cities

Hegra (now Mada'in Saleh) was a very important Nabatean town. It is in Saudi Arabia now. There is a lot of water under the ground here. The Nabateans brought the water up and grew plants and trees. And because the rock was good, they could cut it easily. They built hundreds of houses. They also made large and small buildings and buried dead people in them.

Obodat was one of many Nabatean towns and caravan stations in the Negev Desert. It was on a mountain on the road between Petra and Gaza. Winter rain ran down the mountain, and the Nabateans used this water. They cut places in the rock for it, and built dams. They watered their plants and trees with it. So there was always food and water for the caravans. The name of the town comes from King Obodas 1.

5.1 Were you right?

Look back at Activity 4.4. Then circle the right words in these sentences.

1 In a sandstorm, the camels usually ª *sit down / stand up*. People usually go
ᵇ *behind / on* their animals. Camels always turn their heads ᶜ *away from /
into* the wind and ᵈ *open / shut* their eyes.

2 Petra is in the ª *north / east* of Arabia. Hegra is ᵇ *west of / between* Yathrib
and Petra. Today, Mada'in Saleh is in ᶜ *Iraq / Saudi Arabia* and Petra is in
ᵈ *Egypt / Jordan*.

5.2 What more did you learn?

1 **What does Hassan say to Yazid when the sandstorm comes? Are
these sentences right (✔) or wrong (✗)?**

a ◯ 'We have to run fast, away from the sandstorm. '

b ◯ 'Get on your camel.'

c ◯ 'Go behind your camel.'

d ◯ 'Put your head down.'

e ◯ 'Turn your camel's face away from the wind.'

2 **Answer these questions about the Nabateans. Write *Yes* or *No*.**

a Did they live in the Rub Al-Khali? ....No...

b Did they build beautiful cities? ....

c Did caravans from the south of Arabia have to pay them? ....

d Did they understand the desert very well? ....

e Did they cut buildings into the rock? ....

f Did they build Yazid's city of Qana? ....

g Did they bury important people in large buildings? ....

h Did they have kings? ....

5.3 Language in use

Look at the sentences in the box. Then match the sentences below with the pictures (A–F). After that, make adverbs from these adjectives and finish the sentences.

> We walk **slowly** across the rocky desert.
>
> The camels move **unhappily**.

happy	fast	heavy	slow	loud	quiet

1 ( ) He is driving very .....slowly......

2 ( ) They are playing ....

3 ( ) He is speaking very ....

4 ( ) He is driving ....

5 ( ) It is raining ....

6 ( ) She is shouting ....

5.4 What happens next?

Chapter 5 is 'The End of the Road'. What do you think the traders will do at the end of the road? What will they see? Make notes in your notebook.

The End of the Road

'There are Romans here, and Egyptians, and people from other places too.
I don't understand their languages.'

I am tired. My legs hurt and I want the journey to end. My uncle looks very tired too. He looks older and thinner – but we are all thinner and weaker. We don't always eat well on the road.

'How long is it now?' I ask Hassan.

'From Qana? Three months, I think,' he says. 'But our journey's nearly at an end. You're going to see the sea.'

I think about those months with the caravan. We walked over mountains and across deserts. I saw many strange places, people and things. Our journey took us from the bottom to the top of Arabia – and now we are near the Mediterranean!

Three days later, we arrive at a caravanserai near the sea. Everybody wants to eat and sleep.

Later that day, when the sun is going down, we get up.

There is a lot of noise in the caravanserai. There are people everywhere and the heavy smells of incense and spices are all round us. I can hear a lot of different languages. Some people are wearing very strange clothes.

'Who are those people, Hassan?' I ask. 'And what are they saying?'

'There are Romans here, and Egyptians, and people from other places too. I don't understand their languages.'

The traders put their bags on the ground and open them. They want to sell now because there are a lot of buyers. These buyers want the best frankincense and myrrh. They know that the travellers from the south have fine incense and spices in their bags.

'Go down to the sea, Yazid.' my uncle says. His face is grey. Is he ill, or only tired? 'Trade is the work of men, and I'll be busy. After three months in the desert and the mountains, you'll enjoy seeing the sea again. There are ships from many countries there.'

Hassan and I leave the caravanserai and walk to the sea. There are people everywhere. Some are sitting on the ground and playing games. Some are buying and selling. Other men are talking and laughing. It is the end of a long journey for many people.

'There it is, Hassan – the sea!' I am excited. 'And look at the ships!'

Hundreds of people are carrying big bags onto the ships.

'You two!' a man calls to them. He speaks their language. They turn and look at him. He is selling food. 'Are you hungry? Come and eat,' he says.

They sit down on the ground with some other people and start to eat.

'Are you also from the south, my friends?' he asks.

'Yes, we're with a caravan,' Hassan says with a smile. 'We arrived today.'

'So you came the old way – through the desert!'

'The old way?' I say. 'What do you mean?'

'The future is by sea, friends. Ships are coming up the Red Sea all the time from the south of Arabia and from Abyssinia. And some ships are coming all the way from India. There are no bandits and no sandstorms at sea.'

'Yes,' says another, older man. 'The journeys are easier and cheaper. But our children are desert people. How are they going to live?'

Hassan and I think about the men's words.

'Perhaps I'll go to sea and work on those big ships,' Hassan says. He looks excited. 'Why don't you come too, Yazid? We can see the world.'

I think about my mother and father, my brothers and sisters, at home in Qana.

Then suddenly, a man from our caravan arrives. He is running.

'Yazid – it's your uncle,' he shouts. 'He's very ill. I'm afraid for him. He looks very bad.'

I run to the caravanserai. My uncle is on the floor.

'Uncle!' I cry. 'Are you ill?'

'I'm dying, my boy,' my uncle says, and he sounds very weak. 'I was ill when we left home. But I wanted to make one more journey across the desert. Our family will understand.

'You'll have to be a man and sell my incense and my spices. Then take the money and my camels back to your father. He'll look after your aunt and my children. Will you do that?'

'Yes, Uncle.' I am crying now. 'Of course I'll go home.' In three more months, I will be with my family again.

The next day my uncle dies, and we bury him in the ground near the caravanserai. A week later, the caravan starts the long journey back across the desert.

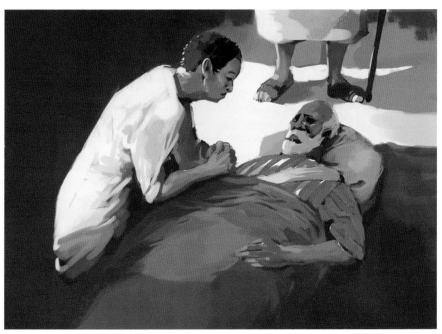

6.1 Were you right?

Look back at your notes in Activity 5.4. Then finish these sentences with the words below.

> ships   caravanserai   three   deserts   sea
> mountains   Rome   Egypt   Mediterranean

The travellers arrive at the end of the road. The journey took
¹ .... months. On the journey they walked across
² .... and went over ³ ....
Now they are at the ⁴ .... Sea. They stop in a
⁵ .... and sleep all day. They see people from
⁶ .... and from ⁷ ....
Sayf starts to sell his incense and spices; Yazid and Hassan walk to the
⁸ .... There are many ⁹ .... there.

6.2 What more did you learn?

Have these conversations.

1 Work with two other students.
You are Yazid, Hassan and the
food seller by the sea. Ask and
answer questions about the
future of the caravan trade.

2 Work with one other student.
You are Yazid and Sayf. What
do you want to say before
Sayf dies?

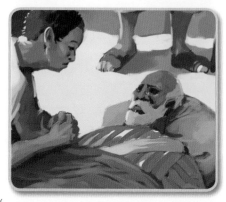

6.3 Language in use

Look at the sentences in the box. Then make one sentence, with *when*, from the sentences below.

> **When** the sun is going down, we get up.
>
> I was ill **when** we left home.

1 We arrived in Gaza. We went to the sea.
    When we arrived in Gaza, we went to the sea .

2 Yazid was excited. He saw the sea.
    .

3 The traders woke up. The buyers arrived.
    .

4 The Romans spoke to Hassan and Yazid. The young men didn't understand.
    .

5 A food-seller called to them. They bought some food.
    .

6 Yazid ran to the caravanserai. He heard about his uncle.
    .

7 Sayf died. They buried him in the desert
    .

6.4 What happens next?

Discuss and make notes. What is next, do you think, for:

Yazid?

the Romans?

the Nabateans?

the cities on the incense road?

the incense and spice trades?

Into the Future

For more than a thousand years, only the people of the desert
knew about many of the beautiful cities of the Nabateans.

After Yazid's journey, the trade in incense and spices changed. In 30 BCE, the Romans took Egypt and brought incense and spices by sea and camel and river to Alexandria.

Later, the Romans took Nabatea too and called it Arabia Petraea. The incense road through the desert was not as important. But the Nabateans didn't stop trading. They built ships, and they carried incense and spices to their cities of Aila and Leuce Come. Trade went by camel to Petra and to the Mediterranean and then to Alexandria by sea. The Roman city of Alexandria was now the most important city for trade on the Mediterranean. When ships arrived, they followed the light from the famous lighthouse, the tallest building in the world at that time.

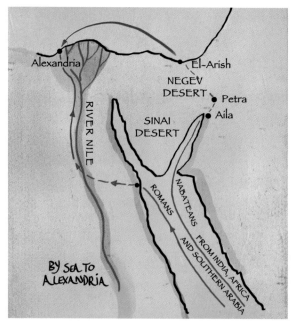

The lighthouse at Alexandria

Why did the Nabateans leave Petra? We don't know. We think that many people left between 300 and 400 CE. We do know that earthquakes were a big problem. They hit Petra in about 363 and 551 CE. Earthquakes also hit other parts of Arabia. Buildings and dams fell. Without water, plants died and people had to leave. For more than a thousand years, only the people of the desert knew about many of the beautiful cities of the Nabateans. Now people study the old buildings, and visitors from other countries can enjoy them.

The famous incense cities of the south also stopped being important. The wall of the Marib dam broke badly in an earthquake in 597 CE. In the years after that, many of the green fields changed to desert sand again.

But for hundreds of years after Yazid's first journey, there was trade in spices and incense across the Mediterranean Sea. There were Arab trading stations in India for spices from the East. Many of these spices came from the Moluccas (Maluku, now in Indonesia). From India, traders took them to Arabia and East Africa.

After Islam started in Arabia and travelled to North Africa, trade between the Arab World and Europe nearly stopped. Fighting in Roman Europe also made trade difficult. Incense and spices cost Europeans more and more. Then trade between Europe and the Middle East began again through the Mediterranean city of Venice. This trade made Venice very rich. But Europeans didn't want to pay middlemen; they wanted *their* ships to bring spices from the East. They knew nothing about the Americas; they knew nothing about the Pacific. They didn't know much about Africa. But they wanted to find the Moluccas. You can see some of their journeys on the next page.

So what happened to the caravan roads of Arabia? Islam brought new life to them. Muslims travelled to Mecca and Madina by camel caravans. Some caravans from Cairo, Istanbul, Baghdad and Damascus were very big; one from Damascus had six thousand people and ten thousand camels! But there weren't many camel caravans by the 1930s. These days, Muslims from round the world arrive in Arabia by road, by sea and by plane.

Journeys of European Ships

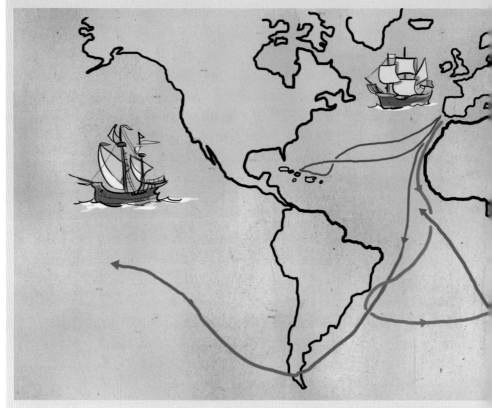

1492–1504 Christopher Columbus travelled west for the King of Spain, and found the Americas.

1497 Vasco da Gama travelled east, round Africa. After his ships arrived in Calicut, in India, Portugal made a lot of money from the spice trade.

1520 More Spanish ships travelled west. Ferdinand Magellan followed Columbus to the Americas, then went south. He found a way to Asia.

1599 The first Dutch ships arrived back in the Netherlands with spices from the East. Later, French and British ships also made their way east and built trading stations for spices.

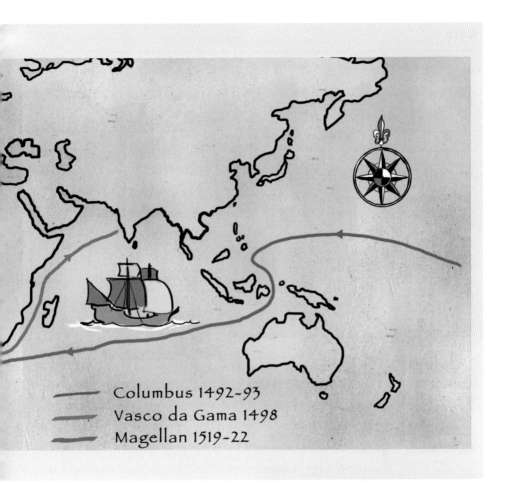

Columbus 1492–93
Vasco da Gama 1498
Magellan 1519–22

In the south of Arabia, the countries of Oman and Yemen were born. The best frankincense in the world today comes from this part of Arabia. Perhaps, more than two thousand years after Yazid travelled with his uncle's caravan, today's incense traders are from his family.

1 **Work with two other students. Plan and then have this conversation in Gaza.**

> Would you like to buy/smell ...?　I've got ... kilos.　It's the best in Arabia.
> Sit down. We can talk about it.　　　It's not expensive.
> A lot of people want this.　　How much do you want?
> It comes from ...　　I can sell it easily.

> Have you got any ...?
> How much have you got?
> Can I smell it?
> I'd like to buy some ...
> Is it good?
> It's very expensive.
> How much is it?
> Can I try some?
> I can buy it cheaper from ...
> I'll give you ... for half a kilo.

Student A　You are a frankincense trader from Qana. You want to sell your frankincense for as much money as possible. You are using Roman money – one *denarius*, a number of *denarii*.

Student B　You are a trader from Rome. You want to buy A's frankincense. You know it is the best in the world. You have to have it. But you don't want to pay much. Can you sell something to this trader too?

Student C　You are an Egyptian trader. You also want to buy A's frankincense. You also know it is the best in the world. You have to have it. But you don't want to pay much. Can you sell something to this trader too?

2 **Now have two other conversations in a city street in your country today. Two students are visitors from another country. Student B and then C are street-sellers. What are you selling? How much money do you want? How much can you get? Can you do better than other students in your class?**

1 Why did people use camels when they travelled across deserts? Write five sentences.

a ....

b ....

c ....

d ....

e ....

2 You want to sell one of your camels. What is good about it? Write the advertisement.

Do you want to buy this camel?

....

....

....

....

....

....

....

....

....

....

....

1 Work with two or three other students. Read about the white oryx. Then read more about it in books or on the Internet. Discuss answers to the questions below.

Arabian white oryx

For hundreds of years, the white oryx lived in the deserts of the Middle East. Then when more guns arrived in Arabia in the 1900s, people killed them for food – and, later, for sport. By the 1960s there weren't many of them. But babies were born in American animal parks. Countries in the Arab world worked with these parks and brought the Arabian oryx back to the deserts in large numbers. About one thousand of them now live in the deserts of Jordan, Saudi Arabia, the United Arab Emirates and Oman. People don't kill them for sport now.

a Why did the number of white oryx fall suddenly in the 1900s?

b How many white oryx lived outside animal parks in 1972?

c How did American animal parks help?

d Which Arabian country has the biggest number of white oryx in its deserts now?

e Why are deserts good homes for the white oryx?

2 **Work with the same students. Choose one of the animals below – or another desert animal. Read about it on the Internet and make notes below.**

What is the name of the animal? ....

Where does it live? ....

Are there many of these animals? ....

What do they eat? ....

Where do they find water? ....

What makes them good desert animals? ....

....

....

....

Arabian wildcat

Arabian wolf

Fennec fox

Arabian jerboa

3 Give a short talk on your desert animal. Listen to other students and ask questions. Make notes in your notebook on one of the other animals.

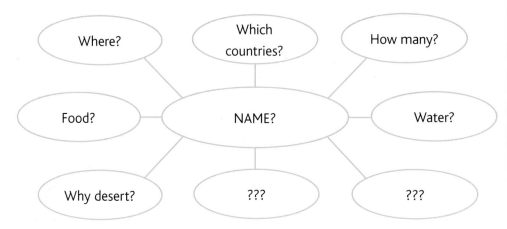

4 Use your notes from exercise 3 and write about that animal.

A desert animal: ....